How and why do animals build homes?

Bobbie Kalman

🌳 **Crabtree Publishing Company**

www.crabtreebooks.com

For my best girl, Kennedy Wilson,
with love from Samantha

Author and editor-in-chief
Bobbie Kalman

Publishing plan research and development
Reagan Miller

Editor
Kathy Middleton

Proofreader
Crystal Sikkens

Photo research
Bobbie Kalman

Design
Bobbie Kalman
Katherine Berti
Samantha Crabtree (cover)

Print and production coordinator
Katherine Berti

Photographs and illustrations
BigStockPhoto: page 6
Dreamstime: pages 5 (top left), 12 (top right)
Thinkstock: pages 1, 9, 17 (bottom), 20 (bottom)
Syaheir Azizan/Shutterstock.com: page 22 (top right)
All other images by Shutterstock

Library and Archives Canada Cataloguing in Publication

Kalman, Bobbie, author
    How and why do animals build homes? / Bobbie Kalman.

(All about animals close-up)
Includes index.
Issued in print and electronic formats.
ISBN 978-0-7787-0544-4 (bound).--ISBN 978-0-7787-0598-7 (pbk.).--
ISBN 978-1-4271-7592-2 (pdf).--ISBN 978-1-4271-7587-8 (html)

1. Animals--Habitations--Juvenile literature. I. Title.

QL756.K354 2014   j591.56'4   C2014-903907-7
                                             C2014-903908-5

Library of Congress Cataloging-in-Publication Data

Kalman, Bobbie.
  How and why do animals build homes? / Bobbie Kalman.
      pages cm -- (All About Animals Close-Up)
  Includes index.
  ISBN 978-0-7787-0544-4 (reinforced library binding) -- ISBN 978-0-7787-0598-7
(pbk.) -- ISBN 978-1-4271-7592-2 (electronic pdf) -- ISBN 978-1-4271-7587-8
(electronic html)
  1. Animals--Habitations--Juvenile literature. I. Title.

QL756.K3554 2015
591.56'4--dc23
                                             2014022879

Crabtree Publishing Company

www.crabtreebooks.com   1-800-387-7650

Printed in the U.S.A./092014/JA20140811

Published in Canada
Crabtree Publishing
616 Welland Ave.
St. Catharines, Ontario
L2M 5V6

Published in the United States
Crabtree Publishing
PMB 59051
350 Fifth Avenue, 59th Floor
New York, New York 10118

Published in the United Kingdom
Crabtree Publishing
Maritime House
Basin Road North, Hove
BN41 1WR

Published in Australia
Crabtree Publishing
3 Charles Street
Coburg North
VIC 3058

Contents

Why build homes?

Homes protect us from bad weather and keep us safe. Animals also build homes for **shelter** and to keep safe from **predators**. Predators are animals that hunt and eat **prey**, or other animals. Many animals build homes to lay eggs or have babies. Some animals build homes for long sleeps called **hibernation**. Homes are also places for animals to make and store food.

*These fox kits, or baby foxes, stay safe in a **den** dug under the ground while their mother looks for food to bring them (see pages 6–7).*

4

This dormouse hibernates, or sleeps deeply, six months of the year in a **nest** made of leaves on the ground.

Honeybees build hives for their eggs, as well as for storing food and making honey (see page 19).

(see page 19)

(see page 9)

What do you think?

Name four reasons why animals build homes. Why do people live in homes?

This prairie dog lives in an underground **burrow** (see page 9).

5

Homes called dens

A den is a shelter inside a hole. It can be a hole in a tree trunk, a tunnel in the ground, or a cave. A den is used as a hiding place from predators. Some dens are made by the animals that live in them, but many dens are natural places that animals find, where they can keep safe.

These coyote pups live in a den among rocks on a mountain.

Hollow trees and logs make great dens for animals like squirrels and the raccoon above. Dens can also be found in oceans. The eels on the right are hiding in a den under some rocks at the bottom of the ocean.

Underground tunnels

Burrows are tunnels that animals dig deep into the ground. Some burrows have several rooms connected by tunnels so many animals can live together. Some are even underwater! Burrows keep animals safe from predators, as well as cold, hot, or wet weather.

This rat is hiding her babies in a burrow.

Homes and towns

Prairie dogs live in big groups. They dig huge burrows called towns, which have many rooms for sleeping and storing food. Above the towns are **grasslands**, or areas covered in grasses and shrubs. Prairie dogs find plenty of grasses and flowers to eat there.

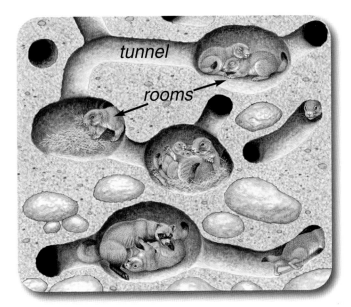

tunnel

rooms

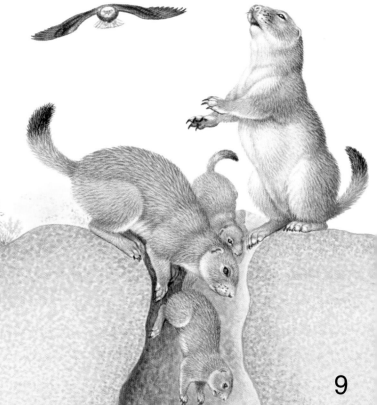

Nests built by birds

Most birds build nests in which they lay their eggs. When the baby birds hatch, or break out of their eggs, they are safe from predators. Most bird parents feed their chicks, or baby birds, until they learn to fly and find their own food.

Some birds build nests in high places, such as trees, chimneys, or the tops of poles. This stork nest is built of sticks at the top of a tree trunk. Behind it are tall mountains.

Sunbird mothers build nests using spider webs to hold the leaves together. Spider silk is very strong.

reeds

Swan parents make their nests on or near water, using plants called reeds. The reed nest is safely hidden by the tall reeds all around it. The cygnets, or swan babies, learn to swim soon after they hatch.

What do you think?

Why is it important for bird parents to build nests? What must baby birds learn to do before they can survive on their own?

Other nest builders

Birds are not the only animals that build nests. Other animals build them, too. Some nests are built for eggs and keeping babies safe. Other nests are used for only a short time, for sleeping.

alligator mother with eggs

Alligators build nests of sticks and mud near water. The mother covers the eggs with plant material to keep them warm. The babies, called hatchlings, make loud calls to their mother when they start to hatch. Their mother digs them out of the nest and carries them to water in her jaws.

Orangutans spend most of their time high up in trees. This orangutan mother makes a new nest of leaves every night on which she and her baby sleep.

Some rabbits build their nests on the ground, using grass and fur. Other rabbits dig burrows called warrens for their babies.

What do you think?

Which of the nests on these pages is the least safe? Why do you think so?

Sea turtle nests

Adult sea turtles live in the ocean. A mother sea turtle makes a nest only when she is ready to lay eggs. She swims back to the same beach where she hatched from an egg. She then crawls along the sand looking for a safe spot to dig an egg chamber, or nest for her eggs. She lays a clutch, or set, of 100 to 150 eggs, usually at night.

After laying her eggs, the sea turtle will cover them with sand and swim away. If predators do not find and eat the eggs first, the hatchlings will dig their way out and crawl to the ocean.

hatchling

eggs

What do you think?

What dangers do the baby turtles face on their way to the ocean? Will they all make it there alive? Why or why not?

Homes in water

eel in sand burrow

This nutria family lives in a burrow on a riverbank.

Many kinds of animals live in oceans, lakes, and rivers. Fish, such as eels, often burrow under the sand at the bottom of the ocean or hide under rocks. Nutrias burrow into the mud on riverbanks. There are two ways to get in and out of the burrows: one in the water and one on land. Babies are safe inside the burrows, and there is plenty of food along the banks of rivers.

Beaver lodges

Beavers build homes called lodges in the deep waters of rivers and lakes. The only way to enter the lodge is underwater. The rooms are high above water, so the beavers can breathe. An extra tunnel is built to escape from a predator that might get in.

These young beavers are chewing branches to add to their lodge.

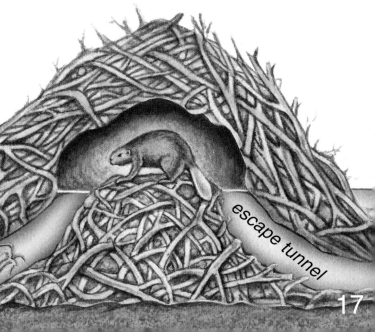

escape tunnel

Farms and factories

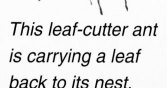

Insects use homes as safe places to lay their eggs and raise their young. Some live and work together to build homes. Ants and other insects also grow and store food the way farmers do.

This leaf-cutter ant is carrying a leaf back to its nest.

*How are ants like farmers? They grow **fungi** as food for their colony, using leaves they collect. A colony is a large group that lives and works together.*

Beehive factories

Beehives are nests, but they are also like factories. A factory makes things that other people use. Honeybees make honey that they, as well as many animals and people, eat. They make honey from nectar, a sweet liquid they gather from flowers. Bees store the nectar in rooms called cells. Other cells contain eggs that will later become honeybees.

Inside a beehive, bees build combs which are structures made up of many cells.

This woman works in a factory that removes honey from honeycombs. The honey will then be put into jars and sold to people.

Amazing structures

vents

More than a million termites may live in this mound! It contains rooms, tunnels, and vents, which are shown in the drawing over the mound.

Termites are insects that build amazing **structures** called **mounds**. Mounds are huge and have many tunnels and rooms. The termites keep their eggs in some rooms and store food in others. The mound has vents, or openings, built in. Vents act as air conditioners and heaters. They can be closed or opened to keep the mound at the same temperature.

Tall homes

Hundreds of people live in tall apartment buildings like this one. The apartments are made up of hallways and rooms. The building has heating and air conditioning. How is this building like a termite mound?

What do you think?

What do you do to make a room cooler when it gets too hot?
How is a hallway like a tunnel?

Built by humans

Humans have constructed the buildings on this page. Which animal homes best match these buildings?

Some people build homes right on water. Which animals live in homes on or under water?

Which animals build homes high up in trees? Why do people build tree houses?

Some people long ago lived in cave homes. Which animals live in homes like these?

Learning more

Books

Saranne, Taylor. *Animal Homes* (Young Architect).
Crabtree Publishing Company, 2015.

Kalman, Bobbie. *Rapping about Animal Homes* (Rapping about...).
Crabtree Publishing Company, 2012.

Kalman, Bobbie. *Homes of living things* (Introducing Living Things).
Crabtree Publishing Company, 2008.

Kalman, Bobbie and John Crossingham. *Insect Homes*
(The World of Insects). Crabtree Publishing Company, 2006.

Websites

Kidport: Reference Library: Animal Homes
www.kidport.com/RefLib/Science/AnimalHomes/AnimalHomes.htm

Highlights Kids: Birds Nest Safari
www.highlightskids.com/audio-story/birds-nest-safari

Youtube: Sea Turtle Nesting Video
www.youtube.com/watch?v=2w5PANyqgnU

Words to know

burrow (BUR-oh) noun A hole or tunnel dug by a small animal as a place to live

den (den) noun A hole made by an animal or one found in nature as a shelter

fungi (FUHN-guy) noun Plantlike living things such as mold

grassland (GRAS-land) noun An area covered in grasses and shrubs

hibernation (HI-ber-ney-shun) noun A deep sleep in which an animal is inactive

mound (mound) noun A hill of soil or earth above the ground. Termites build mounds using soil, saliva, and dung.

nest (nest) noun A home made of twigs, grass, or mud built by animals

predator (PRED-uh-ter) noun An animal that hunts other animals for food

prey (prey) noun An animal that is hunted by another animal

shelter (SHEL-ter) noun A place giving protection from bad weather or enemies

structure (STRUHK-cher) noun Something built or constructed

A noun is a person, place, or thing.

Index

24